THE WONDERFUL WORLD OF WORDS

1

King Norman Nautilus Noun

Dr Lubna Alsagoff

PhD (Stanford)

Marshall Cavendish
Children

King Norman Nautilus Noun was a very good king. But he was also a very proud king.

All of the things in my kingdom are **nouns!**

All of them belong to me.

King Noun liked to say that he owned everything in WOW.

_____ is a noun.

_____ is a noun.

_____ is a noun.

_____ is a noun.

_____ is a noun.

Can you find the nouns in this picture?

3

The king walked out into his huge garden. Everywhere he looked, the king saw nouns.

odlcu

Let's name all the things in the king's garden using nouns.

ilasn

sgrsa

kys

lilh

dpno

eret

subh

kocr

Nouns name things.

It was time for dinner. King Noun saw that all the things around him were nouns.

6

_____ is a noun.

_____ is a noun.

_____ is a noun.

_____ is a noun.

_____ is a noun.

_____ is a noun.

_____ is a noun.

_____ is a noun.

park

beach

river

desert

I own all the places in WOW.

playground

library

castle

school

Nouns also name places.

9

11

Find and colour the 10 nouns in the picture.

cat   candle   bird

book   fork   pencil

leaf   apple   spoon   cup

Everyone in WOW has a lovely ▯▯▯▯▯ .

★ It sounds like "mouse" but it's a place where people live.

When you sleep, you lie on a ▯▯▯ .

★ It sounds like "red" and it's lovely and soft.

The ▯▯▯ was shining!

★ It sounds like "fun" - but it can be very hot!

King Noun said that the ▯▯▯ belonged to him!

★ Clouds live there, and it sounds like 'my'.

It was a beautiful ▯▯▯ in WOW.

★ It sounds like "play" and it's wonderful when the sun shines.

Not far from WOW was a
beautiful green forest, the
Fabulous Forest of WOW.
There, Rabbit lived with
his friends.

The Fabulous
Forest of WOW

R.R. Rabbit

One morning, Rabbit sat up in bed, as he always did, after a long, long sleep. He yawned long and hard until he felt wide awake.

Rabbit looked out of
the window. It was
such a beautiful day!
"I think I'll ask Squirrel
to go for a walk!"

Can you help Rabbit find more wonderful things to say about himself?

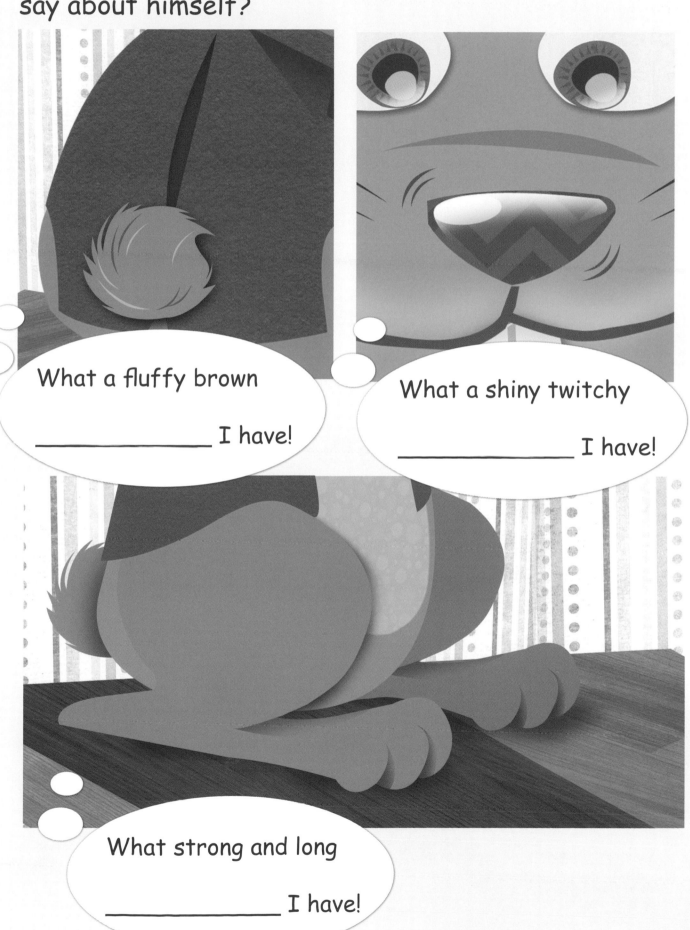

What a fluffy brown

_____ I have!

What a shiny twitchy

_____ I have!

What strong and long

_____ I have!

It was getting late, so Rabbit raced out the door.

Oh dear!

Hello, Squirrel what happened?

And so, Rabbit and Squirrel set off to look for wise old Owl.

END

START

Goodbye!
See you
next time!

Dear Parents,

Welcome to the Wonderful World of Words!

This series of books aims to help children understand grammar in a fun and meaningful way through stories.

WOW teaches children about the different word classes. Learning about word classes is important because it is the first step to building a good foundation in grammar.

Each of these word classes in WOW is represented by a royal character in our kingdom, so children can easily learn about the different types or classes of words, how they are used, and how they interact with other words.

Linked to the story set in the WOW kingdom is another story that is about the animals in the forest of WOW. We'll meet Owl, Rabbit and Squirrel and go on an adventure as they help the animals of WOW learn grammar.

The king begins us on our journey. He is the king, and he is the ruler of all nouns! In this first issue, children learn about nouns.

- Nouns are words that name people, animal, things and places.

Page	Possible Answers
2–3	flower | leaf | apple | bird | sun
4–5	cloud | snail | grass | sky | hill | pond | tree | bush | rock
6–7	chair | table | plate | fork | spoon | cup | glass | teapot
13	house | bed | sun | sky | day
19	tail | nose | legs